# What You Don't Know about Turning 60....

## A Funny Birthday Quiz

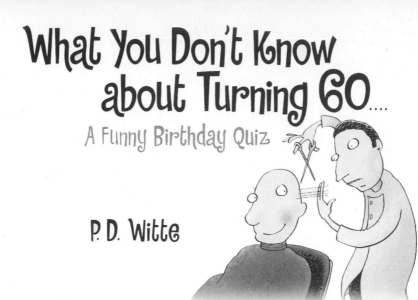

### P. D. Witte

 Meadowbrook Press
Distributed by Simon & Schuster
New York

Library of Congress Cataloging-in-Publication Data

Witte, P. D. (Philip D.)
  What you don't know about turning 60 : a funny birthday quiz / by P.D. Witte.
     p. cm.
  ISBN 0-88166-510-X (Meadowbrook)        ISBN 0-684-04002-6 (Simon & Schuster)
  1. Aging—Humor.  I. Title.
  PN6231.A43W58 2006
  818'.5402—dc22
                              2005022665

Editorial Director: Christine Zuchora-Walske
Coordinating Editor: Megan McGinnis
Proofreader: Angela Wiechmann
Production Manager: Paul Woods
Graphic Design Manager: Tamara Peterson
Cover and Interior Illustrations: Steve Mark

Text © 2006 by P. D. Witte

Published by Meadowbrook Press, 5451 Smetana Drive, Minnetonka, Minnesota 55343

www.meadowbrookpress.com

BOOK TRADE DISTRIBUTION by Simon and Schuster, a division of Simon and Schuster, Inc., 1230 Avenue of the
Americas, New York, New York 10020

10 09 08 07    10 9 8 7 6 5 4 3 2

Printed in the United States of America

# Contents

# Dedication

To Mom

# Acknowledgments

For their thoughtful reviews of this book's content,
Meadowbrook Press thanks the following people:

Loretta Bollman, Jerry Erickson, Valere and Leatte Magnan,
Audrey Mjos, James Pearson, and Tony and Rose Walske.

Chapter 1

# Romance and Sex

**Q:** Can a 60-year-old man have the body of a 30-year-old?

**A:** *If he pays her enough.*

**Q:** How have pharmaceutical advances changed sex for 60-year-olds?

**A:** *Before: She took the pill. Now: He does.*

**Q:** Can a woman nearing age 60 still find her prince?

**A:** *Sure. Ask Camilla, Duchess of Cornwall.*

**Q:** You are a 60-year-old woman and suddenly you feel a heavy weight pressing on your chest. What do you do?

**A:** *Tell your husband to get off you.*

**Q:** Why don't 60-year-old overweight men have bachelor parties?

**A:** *The lap dancers have no place to perform.*

**Q:** How do you flatter 60-year-olds?

**A:** *Ask for proof that they're entitled to a senior discount.*

**Q:** When are 60-year-olds wooed, flattered, and forgotten?

**A:** *Every election season.*

**Q:** How does a 60-year-old woman get nasty with her man?

**A:** *She hides his heart pills.*

**Q:** What does "sex, drugs, and rock-and-roll" mean to a 60-year-old?

**A:** *Taking Viagra while listening to Chubby Checker.*

**Q:** Do 60-year-olds have trysts?

**A:** *Yes. Podiatrists, optometrists, geriatrists.*

**Q:** What passes for bedroom acrobatics when you turn 60?

**A:** *Flipping the mattress over.*

**Q:** What 30th wedding anniversary gift can a man get his wife that'll be sure to please her?

**A:** *Two tickets to Paris—one for her and one for her closest girlfriend.*

**Q:** What's a great pickup line
for people in their 60s?

**A:** *"Wanna date a sexagenarian?"*

**Q:** Any advice for a man seeking a winter-spring romance?

**A:** *Expect to pay more for anything out of season.*

Chapter 2

# Health and Medicine

**Q:** A man's brain starts to shrink after age 60: true or false?

**A:** *True. Now you have another shrinking organ to worry about.*

**Q:** Complete: This is the dawning of the Age of _____.

**A:** *Arthritis.*

**Q:** Where can a 60-year-old ask for—and get—"the usual table"?

**A:** *At the doctor's office, in the examining room.*

**Q:** At age 60, what's worth standing in line for?

**A:** *A flu shot.*

**Q:** Is there a good stretching routine for women in their 60s?

**A:** *Tell people you're in your early 50s. That'd be a stretch.*

**Q:** Any advice for someone concerned about Alzheimer's?

**A:** *Forget about it.*

**Q:** How do 60-year-olds keep track of the days of the week?

**A:** *By the colors of their pills.*

**Q:** Can a doctor's approach to a 60-year-old patient be discomforting?

**A:** *Yes, when it's from the rear and involves a rubber glove.*

**Q:** Where are all 60-year-olds the picture of health?

**A:** *In their high school yearbooks.*

**Q:** For people age 60, what's the difference between giving information and giving too much information?

**A:** *Giving information is referring a friend to your gastroenterologist. Giving too much information is showing your friend a video of your colonoscopy.*

**Q:** A glass or two of fine wine at dinner is good for your health and may even prolong your life: true or false?

**A:** *Absolutely true! (Vintners may send samples to the author in care of the publisher.)*

**Q:** Has medicinal marijuana been used successfully to treat glaucoma?

**A:** *Yes, plus it will make these jokes seem funnier.*

**Q:** What's the most common type of home improvement for 60-year-olds?

**A:** *Building an addition to the medicine cabinet.*

**Q:** Before age 60, you monitor the Dow industrial index. After 60, you monitor what?

**A:** *Your bone density index.*

**Q:** What's a common malady of retired union workers?

**A:** *Pension headaches.*

**Q:** What do some 60-year-olds sink their teeth into every night?

**A:** *Denture cleansing solution.*

# Chapter 3

# Family

**Q:** After giving so much to their children, what are 60-year-old parents entitled to request in return?

**A:** *Grandchildren.*

**Q:** Whom do grandparents visit
to feel younger?

**A:** *Their parents.*

**Q:** What should a 60-year-old man have before starting a second family?

**A:** *Second thoughts.*

**Q:** How do you make a
60-year-old smile?

**A:** *Tell him his cutest grandchild
looks a lot like him.*

**Q:** What do 60-year-olds have in common with their grandchildren?

**A:** *Bedtime and bus fare.*

**Q:** After many years of marriage, can a 60-year-old woman change her husband's ways?

**A:** *That's an old wives' tale.*

**Q:** What's the first question 60-year-olds ask when they visit their children?

**A:** *"Can't you turn up the heat a little?"*

**Q:** Women over 60 are often good flower arrangers: true or false?

**A:** *True—especially women who outlive their husbands.*

**Q:** When does a son stop competing with his father?

**A:** *When he realizes his hairline is receding faster than his father's.*

Chapter 4

# Fashion and Looks

**Q:** What's a punk grandma?

**A:** *A blue-haired lady with a bad attitude.*

**Q:** Where can balding men find realistic-looking hair that matches their own?

**A:** *The shower drain.*

**Q:** Are there any great-looking 60-year-old models?

**A:** *Sure—they were manufactured by Packard, Hudson, Nash, and Studebaker.*

# Q: Are there any 60-year-old runway models?

# A: Yes—DC-4s.

**Q:** Where can you find a group of men who are widely admired, have chiseled good looks, and never seem to age?

**A:** *Mount Rushmore.*

**Q:** He had great success in movies at an early age. He had at least one extreme makeover. He's pushing 80 and still has shiny black hair. Who is he?

**A:** *Mickey Mouse.*

**Q:** Do men age better than women?

**A:** *You wouldn't think so if women wore tuxedos and men had to squeeze into strapless gowns.*

**Q:** Where may a 60-year-old wear a revealing gown?

**A:** *In a hospital.*

**Q:** Is it appropriate for a 60-year-old bride to wear white?

**A:** *Yes—support hose comes in a variety of colors.*

**Q:** What does "hot model" refer to?

**A:** *If you said a sexy young woman or a sports car, you're a man under 60. If you said a condo in Florida with a broken air conditioner, you're at least 60.*

# Chapter 5

# Aging

**Q:** Does anyone yearn to be 60?

**A:** *Yes—people who are 70.*

**Q:** When should you become worried about incidents of forgetfulness?

**A:** *Forgetting your car keys: not a problem. Forgetting your pants: problem.*

**Q:** Do some decisions become easier once you reach 60?

**A:** *Well, if you ever win the lottery, you'll know to take the lump sum, not the annual payments.*

**Q:** What three words will flatter a 60-year-old, and what three words will depress a 60-year-old?

**A:** *"You look great" and "for your age."*

**Q:** When do you know it's time to buy a hearing aid?

**A:** *When the burglar alarm goes off and you check to see who's ringing the doorbell.*

**Q:** What's a 60-year-old who takes out a 30-year mortgage?

**A:** *An optimist.*

**Q:** Why should 60-year-olds be grateful for Benjamin Franklin's accomplishments?

**A:** *He invented bifocals and the rocking chair, and he proved that chubby bald guys can be sexy.*

**Q:** What do the following have in common if you're a 60-year-old male: winter, river, and your last name?

**A:** *Each may be preceded by "Old Man."*

**Q:** Can carbon be used to date people?

**A:** Yes. *If a person knows how to use carbon paper, he or she is at least middle-aged.*

**Q:** Can a 60-year-old's brain function like a computer?

**A:** *Sure. After a few minutes of inactivity, it goes into sleep mode.*

**Q:** What do the following have in common: hips, knees, senior management?

**A:** *All can be replaced.*

**Q:** Ice, iron, stone, and steam are all what?

**A:** *Ages older than you are.*

**Q:** How is it that mimes can continue to perform into their 60s?

**A:** *They don't have to worry about remembering their lines.*

**Q:** What do you call a 60-year-old ironworker?

**A:** *An elder welder.*

**Q:** What is one of the ironies of aging for men?

**A:** *As time passes, they have less hair to cut, but the price of haircuts keeps increasing.*

**Q:** What do older people and older homes have in common?

**A:** *In bad weather their joints creak.*

**Q:** When does a trip to the post office seem to take forever?

**A:** *When you're behind a 60-year-old who's trying to decide between the flag stamps and the flower stamps.*

**Q:** Crazy + money + age = _____?

**A:** *Eccentric.*

**Q:** What do older people and aged cheeses sometimes have in common?

**A:** *Prominent blue veins.*

**Q:** What is the aging algorithm?

**A:** *Every 10 years, your chin doubles.*

Chapter 6

# Recreation

**Q:** What is "easy listening" for a 60-year-old?

**A:** *Any conversation with someone who speaks slowly, clearly, and loudly.*

**Q:** Do 60-year-olds like Napster?

**A:** *Yes, especially in the afternoonster.*

**Q:** How can you spot a 60-year-old redneck?

**A:** *He has a gun rack on his rocking chair.*

**Q:** What's the most anticipated meal in the lives of 60-year-olds?

**A:** *The retirement dinner.*

**Q:** What's a senior screwdriver?

**A:** *Orange juice and Metamucil.*

**Q:** Why is the aging process like skiing?

**A:** *Both involve long downhill slides.*

**Q:** What do the following have in common for a 60-year-old: an opera, a neighbor's slide show, and the Tunnel of Love?

**A:** *All are nap opportunities.*

**Q:** Should a 60-year-old invest in a time-share on the beach?

**A:** *Only as a last resort.*

**Q:** What is the ultimate driving machine for 60-year-olds?

**A:** *A BMW with tail fins.*

**Q:** What is the most popular destination for 60-year-old air travelers?

**A:** *The airplane bathroom.*

**Q:** What do you call a 60-year-old who competes in Iron Man contests?

**A:** *Rusty.*

**Q:** Do oldsters like low-stakes gambling?

**A:** *Bingo!*

**Q:** Boston Red Sox, Chicago White Sox, Los Angeles _____?

**A:** *Botox.*

**Q:** What is "house music" to a 60-year-old?

**A:** *The theme song to Art Linkletter's old TV show.*

**Q:** What one word shouted by a 60-year-old can cause everyone around to cringe in fear?

**A:** *"Fore!"*

**Q:** What qualifies as acrobatics for a 60-year-old?

**A:** *A stock split.*

**Q:** Complete this sentence:
The early bird...

**A:** *...dinner special is from
5:00 to 6:00* P.M.

**Q:** Why do 60-year-olds ask to see a menu before entering a restaurant?

**A:** *To see if the print is large enough to read.*

**Q:** What is prime time for 60-year-olds?

**A:** *About 30 years ago.*

**Q:** Are there any 60-year-old comic book superheroes?

**A:** *The Gray Lantern, Hot Flash Gordon, and Supergramps.*

Chapter 7

# Looking Back /
# When You Were Young

**Q:** How did kids fresh out of high school in the 1960s manage to tour Asia for months at a time on practically no money?

**A:** *They got drafted.*

**Q:** Most people age 60 know
at least one word of Russian.
What is that word?

**A:** *Sputnik.*

**Q:** Was U.S. geography easier to learn when 60-year-olds were in school?

**A:** *Yes. They had to memorize only 48 state capitals.*

**Q:** Sunshine and Moonbeam are examples of what?

**A:** *Common names of children born to hippie-era parents.*

**Q:** What replaced the Cold War as the biggest fear among people age 60?

**A:** *Cold bathrooms.*

**Q:** How can 60-year-olds increase the value of their homes?

**A:** *By converting their underground bomb shelters into wine cellars.*

**Q:** Who was "Ike" in "I like Ike"?

**A:** *Dwight D. Eisenhower. If you said Ike Turner, you're probably younger than 60.*

**Q:** Whom were political activists protesting against in the 1960s, and whom are they protesting against today?

**A:** *A President from Texas.*

**Q:** What do singers Little Richard and Little Anthony have in common?

**A:** *They are both now little old men.*

**Q:** How do 60-year-olds determine if a car is an antique?

**A:** *If they were too young to drive it when the model was introduced, it's an antique.*